■SCHOLASTIC

WRITING PRACTICE

D1571582

New York • Toronto • London • Auckland • Sydney
Mexico City • New Delhi • Hong Kong • Buenos Aires

Teaching *Resources*

Cover design by Jay Namerow
Interior illustrations by Micheal Denman
Interior design by Quack & Company

ISBN 0-439-81912-1

2 3 4 5 6 7 8 9 10 40   13 12 11 10 09 08 07

Table of Contents

Dear Parent:

Welcome to *3rd Grade Writing Practice!* This valuable tool is designed to help your child succeed in school. Scholastic, the most trusted name in learning, has been creating quality educational materials for school and home for nearly a century. And this resource is no exception.

Inside this book, you'll find colorful and engaging activity pages that will give your child the practice he or she needs to master essential skills, such as identifying sentences and fragments, capitalizing and punctuating sentences, expanding sentences, building paragraphs, and so much more.

To support your child's learning experience at home, try these helpful tips:

- Provide a comfortable, well-lit place to work, making sure your child has all the supplies he or she needs.

- Encourage your child to work at his or her own pace. Children learn at different rates and will naturally develop skills in their own time.

- Praise your child's efforts. If your child makes a mistake, offer words of encouragement and positive help.

- Display your child's work and celebrate his successes with family and friends.

We hope you and your child will enjoy working together to complete this workbook.

Happy learning!
The Editors

Dinnertime

A **sentence** is a group of words that expresses a complete thought.
A **fragment** is an incomplete thought.

Write *S* for sentence or *F* for fragment.

_____ 1. Insects eat many different things.

_____ 2. Some of these things.

_____ 3. The praying mantis eats other insects.

_____ 4. Water bugs eat tadpoles and small frogs.

_____ 5. Flower nectar makes good.

_____ 6. Build nests to store their food.

_____ 7. The cockroach will eat almost anything.

_____ 8. Termites.

_____ 9. A butterfly caterpillar.

_____ 10. Bite animals and people.

_____ 11. Some insects will even eat paper.

_____ 12. Insects have different mouth parts to help them eat.

On another piece of paper, write about three things you did during the day using only sentence fragments. Have someone read it. Did they understand it? Why or why not?

A Real Meal

 A **sentence** *is a group of words that expresses a complete thought.*

Change each fragment from page 5 to a sentence by adding words from the Bug Box. Remember to use a capital letter at the beginning and a period at the end of each sentence.

1. _____

2. _____

3. _____

4. _____

5. _____

6. _____

are wood eaters.

Mosquitoes

are wood, plants, and nectar.

eats leaves.

food for bees.

Wasps

 On another piece of paper, write a fragment about your favorite dinner. Then change it into a sentence.

Rock Your World

 A telling sentence is called a **statement**.
A statement begins with a capital letter and ends with a period.

Rocks

There are three types of rocks.   one type is called

igneous   These are rocks that were made by

volcanoes.   Another kind is called sedimentary.   they

are formed by layers of rocks, plants, and animals   The

last type of rock is called metamorphic.   They are

rocks that change because of heat and pressure.

rocks are found everywhere in our world

Find the three statements that are missing a capital letter and a period. Rewrite the three statements correctly.

1. _____

2. _____

3. _____

Rock and Roll

 A statement is used to answer a question.

Use a complete sentence to write the answer
to each question.

1. **How many types of rocks are on our planet? (three)**

   There are three types of rocks on our planet.

2. **How hot is the melted rock inside the earth? (more than 2000°F)**

   _____

3. **Where are most igneous rocks formed? (inside the earth)**

   _____

4. **What type of rock is marble? (metamorphic)**

   _____

5. **In what type of rock are fossils found? (sedimentary)**

   _____

Wacky World

An asking sentence is called a **question**. It begins with a capital letter and ends with a question mark (**?**).

Write each question correctly.

1. why is that car in a tree

_____

2. should that monkey be driving a bus

_____

3. did you see feathers on that crocodile

_____

4. can elephants really lay eggs

_____

5. is that my mother covered in spots

_____

On another piece of paper, draw your own picture of a wacky world. Write two questions about your picture.

The Real World

A question begins with a capital letter and ends with a question mark (?). It often begins with one of the words listed below.

Who	*When*
Will	*Can*
What	*Why*
Would	*Did*
Where	*How*
Should	*Is*

Imagine that you are interviewing your favorite famous person (for example, an actor, a president, or a rock star). Write five questions you would ask this person. Use a different beginning word for each question.

I am interviewing _____.

1. _____

2. _____

3. _____

4. _____

5. _____

On another piece of paper, write an answer to each question.

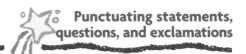

The Dry Desert

 A sentence that shows strong feeling or excitement is called an **exclamation**. *It ends with an exclamation point (!).*

Finish each sentence with a period, a question mark, or an exclamation point.

1. It is hard for plants and animals to get water in the desert

2. Can a cactus live without enough water

3. Some deserts are hot, and others are cool

4. A lizard is running toward us

5. Does a camel really store water in its hump

6. Some deserts are cold and covered with ice

7. How often does it rain in the desert

8. The largest desert is the Sahara

9. Are there any deserts in the United States

10. There is a long snake slithering across the sand

11. People who live in the desert travel to find water

12. I see water up ahead

 **Read these two sentences aloud: I hear a noise. I hear a noise!
How does your voice change when you read an exclamation?**

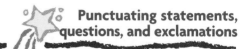
The Sunny Sahara

➡️ *Every sentence begins with a capital letter.*
A statement ends with a period.
A question ends with a question mark.
An exclamation ends with an exclamation point.

Write each sentence correctly.

1. the Sahara Desert is in Africa

_____

2. do people live in the Sahara Desert

_____

3. the Sahara Desert is about the same size as the United States

_____

4. how high is the temperature in the Sahara Desert

_____

5. once the temperature reached 138°F

_____

 On another piece of paper, write a sentence with two mistakes. Ask a friend to circle the mistakes.

A Snowy Scene

 Complete:

Every sentence begins with a _____.

A statement ends with a _____.

A question ends with a _____.

An exclamation ends with an _____.

Write two statements, questions, and exclamations about the picture.

Statements:

1. _____

2. _____

Questions:

1. _____

2. _____

Exclamations:

1. _____

2. _____

 On another piece of paper, turn this statement into a question and an exclamation: It snowed ten inches last night.

A Snowy Story

 *After you write a sentence, go back and look for mistakes. This is called **proofreading** your work.*

Use these proofreading marks to correct 11 mistakes in the story.

<u>mars</u> = **Make a capital letter.**   (?) = **Add a question mark.**

(•) = **Add a period.**   (!) = **Add an exclamation point.**

Snow Day

the kids at Elm School had been waiting for a snowstorm? they knew school would be canceled if the storm brought a lot of snow last week their wish came true it snowed 12 inches school was canceled, and the kids spent the day sledding, building snowmen, and drinking hot chocolate. it was a great snow day

Find two sentences that had two mistakes and write them correctly.

1. <u>   </u>

2. <u>   </u>

 On another piece of paper, write a sentence with two mistakes. Ask a friend to find the mistakes.

Sentences That Slither

 *A sentence tells about someone or something. This is called the **subject**.*

Write the letter to show the subject of each sentence.

A. The short blind snake

B. Tree snakes

C. The flowerpot snake

D. Bird snakes

E. A pit viper snake

F. All snakes

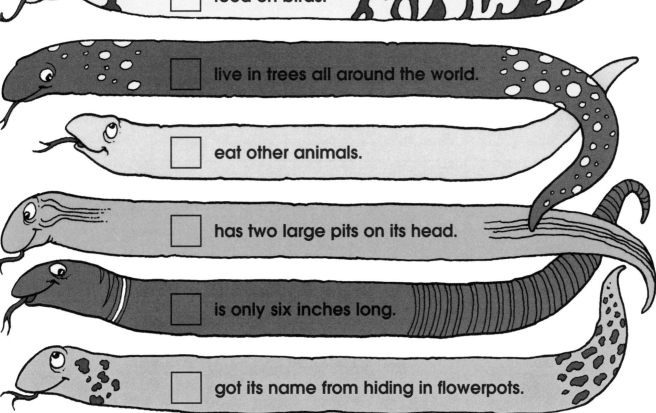

☐ feed on birds.

☐ live in trees all around the world.

☐ eat other animals.

☐ has two large pits on its head.

☐ is only six inches long.

☐ got its name from hiding in flowerpots.

 Confuse someone at home! Leave out the subject part of two sentences at dinner. Can they understand?

A Reptile Fact Sheet

 A sentence tells what the subject does or is. This part of the sentence is called the **verb**.

Use the list of subjects as the beginning for eight sentences. Then add a verb to tell what the subject is doing.

Snakes

Lizards

Crocodiles

Turtles

Dinosaurs

Iguanas

Alligators

Pythons

1. _____

2. _____

3. _____

4. _____

5. _____

6. _____

7. _____

8. _____

 On another piece of paper, write three sentences about your favorite things to do after school. Circle the verb in each sentence.

Stretching Sentences

 A sentence is more interesting when it includes more than just a subject and a verb. It may tell where or when the sentence is happening. It may also tell why something is happening.

Write a sentence describing each set of pictures. Include a part that tells where, why, or how something is happening.

1. _____

2. _____

3. _____

4. _____

 Find a cartoon in the newspaper. Use the pictures to write a sentence on another piece of paper that includes a subject, a verb, and a part that tells where, when, or why.

Stretch It!

 A sentence includes a subject and a verb. A sentence is more interesting when it also includes a part that tells where, when, or why.

Add more information to each sentence by telling where, when, or why. Write the complete new sentence.

1. Mom is taking us shopping.

_____

2. The stores are closing.

_____

3. We need to find a gift for Dad.

_____

4. I will buy new jeans.

_____

5. We may eat lunch.

_____

 Find two sentences in your favorite book that include a subject, verb, and a part that tells where, when, or why. Write the sentences on another piece of paper.

Ketchup and Mustard

Sometimes two sentences can be combined to make one sentence.

Sentences that share the same subject seem to go together like ketchup and mustard. Rewrite the sentences by combining their endings with the word *and*.

1. I ordered a hamburger.
I ordered a milkshake.

I ordered a hamburger and a milkshake.

2. I like salt on my French fries.
I like ketchup on my French fries.

_____

3. My mom makes great pork chops.
My mom makes great applesauce.

_____

4. My dad eats two huge helpings of meat loaf!
My dad eats two huge helpings of potatoes!

_____

5. My brother helps set the table.
My brother helps clean the dishes.

_____

6. We have cookies for dessert.
We have ice cream for dessert.

_____

Let's Eat Out!

 *Two sentences can be combined to make one sentence by using the words **although**, **after**, **because**, **until**, and **while**.*

Choose a word from the menu to combine the two sentences into one sentence.

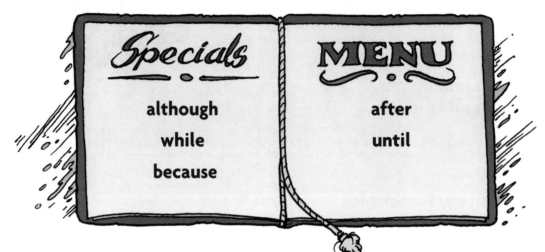

Specials

although

while

because

MENU

after

until

1. We are eating out tonight. Mom worked late.

_____

2. We are going to Joe's Fish Shack. I do not like fish.

_____

3. Dad said I can play outside. It's time to leave.

_____

4. We can play video games. We are waiting for our food.

_____

5. We may stop by Ida's Ice Cream Shop. We leave the restaurant.

_____

 Read the back of a cereal box. Find two sentences that could be combined.

Buckets of Fun

 A **describing word** *helps you imagine how something looks, feels, smells, sounds, or tastes.*

Write a list of describing words on each bucket to fit the bucket's category.

words that describe size

_____

_____

_____

words that describe taste or smell

_____

_____

words that describe sounds

_____

_____

words that describe how something feels

_____

_____

_____

words that describe weather

_____

_____

words that describe feelings

_____

_____

 Make a "mystery bag" by putting a secret object inside. Tell someone at home about the object inside using describing words!

At the Beach

 A **describing word** *makes a sentence more interesting.*

Read the describing words found in the beach balls. Add the describing words to make each sentence more interesting. Write each new sentence.

1. The snow cone sat in the sun.

_____

2. Many children ran toward the ocean waves.

_____

3. My friends built a sand castle.

_____

4. My brother grabbed his beach toys.

_____

5. Our dog tried to catch beach balls.

_____

 On another piece of paper, draw a beach ball. Fill it with words that describe a day at the beach.

The Great Outdoors

 A **describing word** can tell more about a subject or a verb.

Add describing words to make each sentence more interesting.

1. The _____ hikers walked back to camp _____.

2. The _____ bird sang _____.

3. The _____ tree grew _____.

4. _____ children played _____.

5. My _____ sister swam _____.

6. The _____ crickets chirped _____.

7. The _____ flowers bloomed _____.

8. The _____ swing set creaked _____.

9. The _____ ice cream melted _____.

10. The _____ trees shook _____ in the storm.

 Where do you like to spend time outside? On another piece of paper, write the name of your favorite outdoor place. Then write three words that describe it.

Outdoor Excitement

 A **describing word** *can be added to a sentence.*

red

☐ = **Add a describing word.** She wore a ∧ dress.

Read the sentences about each picture. Then use proofreading marks to add a describing word to each sentence.

1. The girl picked flowers.

2. The girl swatted the bees.

3. A bee stung the girl.

1. The boy played a game.

2. The boy won a trophy.

3. The boy held his trophy.

 Add two describing words to this sentence: The campers heard a sound in the night.

Crazy Cartoons

 A story is more interesting when the characters talk with one another.

Use the speech bubbles to show what each character is saying.

 Cut a comic strip from the newspaper. Glue it to another piece of paper and make large speech bubbles. Rewrite the cartoon with your own words.

What Did She Say?

 Quotation marks (" ") *are used to show a character is talking in a story. They surround only the character's words.*

Fill in the speech bubbles to match the paragraph below each picture.

Daisy put on her rain boots, coat, and hat. "I think it's fun to splash in the puddles," she said.

As the rain continued, the puddles turned to streams. "Rain, rain, don't go away!" Daisy sang.

"Wow! I should have worn my bathing suit!" Daisy shouted as the water rose higher.

Then Daisy had an idea. She turned her umbrella upside down and climbed in. "It's a perfect day to go sailing," she said.

 Ask someone at home for an old photograph of yourself and someone else. Glue it to another piece of paper and make speech bubbles to show what you may have been saying when the picture was taken.

Look Who's Talking!

 Quotation marks surround a character's exact words. In a statement, use a comma to separate the character's exact words from the rest of the sentence. In a question and an exclamation, use the correct ending punctuation after the character's exact words.

Statement: "I have to go now," said my friend.
Question: "Where are you?" asked my mom.
Exclamation: "Wow!" the boy exclaimed.

Write a sentence to match each speech bubble. Use the examples above to help you.

 On another piece of paper, write a conversation you had with a friend during the day. Use quotation marks to show what you and your friend each said.

Chitchat

 Quotation marks can be added to a story using these proofreading marks.

<u>m</u>ars = **Make a capital letter.**   (?) = **Add a question mark.**   (!) = **Add an exclamation point.**

(.) = **Add a period.**   (,) = **Add a comma.**   (")(") = **Add quotation marks.**

Find 16 mistakes in the story. Use proofreading marks to correct them.

Lucky Day

Drew woke up early on Saturday. No school today, he said He found

his mom working in the garden What are you doing ” he asked.

“I am planting these flowers, she answered.

Drew looked down He couldn't believe it. A four-leaf clover” he shouted

“This should help us win our big game today he said.

Drew's entire day was perfect. his sister shared her toys, the ice-cream

truck brought his favorite flavor, and his team won the big game “What a

day! he whispered to himself as he fell asleep that night.

 On another piece of paper, write about your luckiest day. Include at least two sets of quotation marks.

Under the Big Top

 Sentences can be written in order of beginning (B), middle (M), and ending (E) to make a paragraph.

Write a middle and ending sentence to complete each paragraph.

B **The circus started with a roll of drums and flashing lights.**

M Next, _____

E Last, _____

B **The tightrope walker stepped into the spotlight.**

M Next, _____

E Last, _____

B **The lion tamer came on stage.**

M Next, _____

E Last, _____

B **The dancing ponies appeared in the center ring.**

M Next, _____

E Last, _____

A Circus Train

 Sometimes a paragraph tells a story.

Write three sentences about each set of pictures to make a short story paragraph.

_____

_____

_____

_____

_____

_____

_____

_____

 Read your paragraphs to a friend.

Terrific Topics

 *A **paragraph** is a group of sentences that tells about one idea called the **topic**.*

Imagine that you are planning to write a paragraph about each topic below. Write three ideas for each topic.

gardening	fish	homework
1. flowers	1.	1.
2. vegetables	2.	2.
3. pesky insects	3.	3.
summer sports	**friends**	**favorite books**
1.	1.	1.
2.	2.	2.
3.	3.	3.
favorite movies	**American history**	**healthy foods**
1.	1.	1.
2.	2.	2.
3.	3.	3.

It Just Doesn't Belong!

 *The sentence that tells the topic of a paragraph is called the **topic sentence***.

Draw a line through the sentence that does not belong with the topic.

Topic: Dogs make great family pets.

Dogs have great hearing, which helps them protect a family from danger.

Most dogs welcome their owners with wagging tails.

My favorite kind of dog is a boxer.

Many dogs are willing to play with children in a safe manner.

Topic: The history of the American flag is quite interesting.

The first American flag had no stars at all.

Not much is known about the history of Chinese flags.

Historians cannot prove that Betsy Ross really made the first American flag.

The American flag has changed 27 times.

Topic: Hurricanes are called by different names depending on where they occur.

Hurricanes have strong, powerful winds.

In the Philippines, hurricanes are called baguios.

Hurricanes are called typhoons in the Far East.

Australian people use the name willy-willies to describe hurricanes.

 Read a paragraph from a favorite chapter book. Read the topic sentence to someone at home.

Missing Topics

 A topic sentence is sometimes called the **main idea**.

Read the groups of sentences. Then write a topic
sentence that tells the main idea of the paragraph.

_____

_____

One reason is that guinea pigs do not usually bite. Second, guinea pigs don't

make as much noise as other rodents might during the night. Last, they are

large enough that they can be found if they ever get lost in a house.

_____

_____

First, spread peanut butter on two pieces of bread. Next, cut a banana into

slices and lay them on top of the peanut butter. Then close the two pieces of

bread into a sandwich. Last, eat up!

_____

_____

Frogs usually have longer legs and wetter skin than toads do. Many frogs live

near a water source of some kind while toads prefer a damp, muddy

environment. Frog eggs and toad eggs are different in shape.

 **On another piece of paper, make a list of three subjects you know a lot about. Write a
possible topic sentence for each of the subjects.**

Try These Topics

*Writing a topic sentence takes thought because your
entire paragraph must follow the main idea.*

Write a topic sentence for each subject.

1. My Chores

_____

2. The Best Book Ever

_____

3. My Favorite After-School Activity

_____

4. Appropriate TV Shows for Kids

_____

5. Types of Coins

_____

6. Our Greatest Presidents

_____

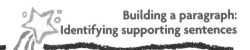

That Drives Me Crazy!

 The sentences that follow the topic sentence tell more about the topic. They are called **supporting sentences**.

Read the paragraph below. Cross out the three sentences that do not support the topic.

My Pet Peeves

I am a pretty agreeable person, but there are a few things around my house that drive me crazy. One such thing is when my younger brothers go into my bedroom and destroy my building creations. My three-year-old brothers both have blonde hair. I also get upset when my sister sings at the dinner table. Her favorite sport is gymnastics. My greatest pet peeve is when my older brother taps his pencil on the kitchen table while I am studying spelling words. I wish I had a fish tank in my room. My brothers and sister are really great, but there are moments when they make me crazy!

Rewrite the paragraph above skipping the sentences that you crossed out. The new paragraph should have one topic sentence followed by the supporting sentences.

_____

_____

_____

_____

_____

_____

Do You Agree?

 The supporting sentences in a paragraph tell more about the topic.

Write three supporting sentences to complete each paragraph.

Shorter Weeks

I think the school week should be shortened to four days for three

reasons. The first reason is _____

_____

_____. Another reason is _____

_____

_____. The last reason is _____

_____

_____. I think four-day

weeks just make more sense!

Looking Back:

Now proofread your paragraph for:

    capital letters and periods

    complete sentences

    describing words

    sentences that support the topic

 **On another piece of paper, write a paragraph that begins with this topic sentence:
I think I should be able to stay up later for three reasons.**

A Great Trick

➡ *The supporting sentences should be in an order that makes sense.*

Read the topic sentence, then number the supporting ideas first (1) to last (4).

Last week I played a great trick on my mom.

_____ won a huge rubber snake

_____ went to a carnival

_____ called my mom outside

_____ put snake in my mom's flower garden

Now use the topic sentence and ideas in the correct order to write a paragraph telling the story. Be sure to use complete sentences.

_____

_____

_____

_____

_____

_____

Think of a trick you have played on someone. On another piece of paper, write a topic sentence and three supporting sentences about the trick.

Good to Know

 A good paragraph has at least three supporting sentences.

Finish the paragraphs below by writing three sentences that support each topic sentence.

Airplanes are useful in many ways. First, _____

_____.

Second, _____

_____.

Third, _____

_____.

Life as a child today is quite different from the way it was when my

parents were young. First, _____

_____.

Second, _____

_____.

Third, _____

_____.

Clip a topic sentence from a magazine or newspaper article. Glue it to another piece of paper and write three supporting sentences.

Closing Time!

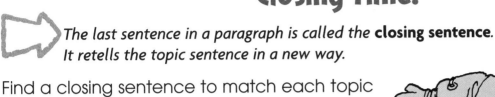

*The last sentence in a paragraph is called the **closing sentence**. It retells the topic sentence in a new way.*

Find a closing sentence to match each topic sentence. Write the closing sentence.

Closing Sentences

Some gardeners in Florida and Texas can enjoy their flowers all year long.

Of all the seasons, autumn is the best.

Life would never be the same without computers.

There are many subjects in school, but math is the most difficult.

Though dangerous, the job of an astronaut is exciting.

---

1. **Fall is my favorite season in the year.**

2. **Astronauts have one of the most exciting and dangerous jobs.**

_____

3. **Math is the toughest part of our school curriculum.**

_____

4. **Many types of flowers grow year-round in the southern states.**

_____

5. **Computer technology has changed many aspects of our lives.**

_____

That's All Folks!

 *The **closing sentence** retells the topic sentence or main idea of a paragraph.*

Write a closing sentence for each paragraph.

All cyclists should wear helmets while riding their bikes. Many injuries occur to the head in biking accidents. Helmets could help prevent the injuries. Helmets also make cyclists more easily noticed by car drivers. _____

_____

There are many things to do on a rainy day. If you like to write, you could send a letter to a friend or make a book. If you prefer craft projects, you could make a bookmark or a collage. If you really enjoy games, you could play cards or build a puzzle. _____

_____

The wheel must be one of the world's most important inventions. First, we would have no means of transportation if it were not for wheels. Second, we would not be able to enjoy many of our favorite pastimes, like in-line skating and riding a bike. Last, it would be very difficult to move heavy objects around without wheels. _____

_____

A Paragraph Plan

Follow these steps in planning a paragraph.
1. Choose a topic (main idea).
2. Brainstorm ideas about the topic. (You will need at least three.)
3. Write a topic sentence.
4. Write a closing sentence by retelling the topic sentence.

Follow this plan to write a paragraph about Ben Franklin.

1. Ben Franklin

2. a) inventor of bifocal eyeglasses and Franklin stove
b) scientist who proved that lightning is electricity
c) involved in writing the Declaration of Independence

3. Ben Franklin was a man of many talents.

4. Ben Franklin displayed his talents in many ways.

_____

_____

_____

_____

_____

_____

_____

_____

_____

Read your paragraph to yourself. Then add a describing word to each supporting sentence.

My Very Own Paragraph

 Use a paragraph plan before you begin writing.

It is time to plan and write your own paragraph. You may want to use your own topic or one of the following topics: My Favorite Vacation, Collecting Coins, Our Pet Snake.

1. Choose a topic. _____

2. Brainstorm three supporting ideas.

    a) _____

    b) _____

    c) _____

3. Write a topic sentence. _____

4. Write a closing sentence. _____

Use the plan to write your own paragraph.

_____

_____

_____

_____

_____

_____

_____

_____

Do I Have a Story for You!

 *A paragraph that tells a story is called a **narrative paragraph**. Its supporting sentences tell what happen at the beginning, middle, and end. A **story map** helps you plan the story's setting, characters, problem, and solution.*

Write a sentence about each part of the map. Then complete the plan for a narrative paragraph using the story map.

Beginning	**Middle**	**End**

setting and characters → problem → solution

_____ _____ _____

_____ _____ _____

_____ _____ _____

1. Write a topic sentence. _____

_____

2. Write a supporting sentence for the beginning, middle, and end.

B _____

M _____

E _____

3. Write a closing sentence. _____

_____

 On another piece of paper, use the plan to write a narrative paragraph.

Map It Out

 Use a story map to help plan a narrative paragraph before you begin writing.

Draw pictures to complete the map. Then use it to write a narrative paragraph.

Beginning	**Middle**	**End**
setting and characters	problem	solution

1. Write a topic sentence. _____

   _____

2. Write a supporting sentence for the beginning, middle, and end.

   B _____

   M _____

   E _____

3. Write a closing sentence. _____

   _____

 On another piece of paper, use the plan to write a narrative paragraph.

I'm Sure You'll Agree!

 A **persuasive paragraph** gives your opinion and tries to convince the reader to agree. Its supporting ideas are reasons that back up your opinion.

Topic sentence
→ Our family should have a dog for three reasons.

Reason 1

First, pets teach responsibility. If we get a dog, I will feed him and take him for walks after school. The second reason for having a pet is that he would ← *Reason 2* make a good companion for me when everyone else is busy. I won't drive Dad crazy always asking him to play catch with me. The third ← *Reason 3* reason we need a dog is for safety. He would warn us of danger and keep our house safe. For all of these reasons, I'm sure you'll agree that we should jump in the car and head toward the adoption agency right away. I don't know how we have made it this long without a dog! ← *closing sentence*

Plan and write a persuasive paragraph asking your parents for something (such as a family trip, expensive new shoes, or an in-ground pool).

1. Choose a topic. _____

2. Write a topic sentence. _____

3. Brainstorm three supporting reasons.

Reason 1 _____

Reason 2 _____

Reason 3 _____

 On another piece of paper, use your plan to write a persuasive paragraph.

That's a Fact!

 An **expository paragraph** *provides facts or explains ideas. The supporting sentences give more details about the topic.*

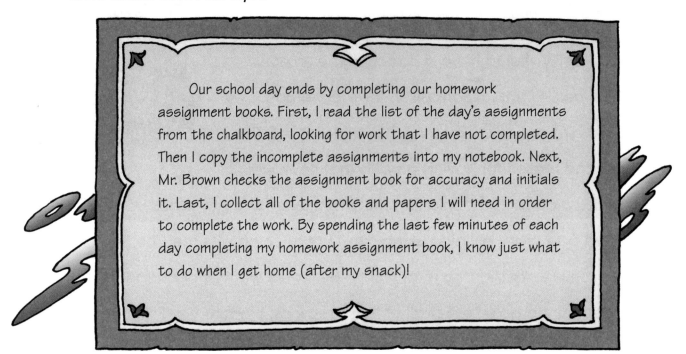

Our school day ends by completing our homework assignment books. First, I read the list of the day's assignments from the chalkboard, looking for work that I have not completed. Then I copy the incomplete assignments into my notebook. Next, Mr. Brown checks the assignment book for accuracy and initials it. Last, I collect all of the books and papers I will need in order to complete the work. By spending the last few minutes of each day completing my homework assignment book, I know just what to do when I get home (after my snack)!

Plan an expository paragraph explaining one part of your school day.

Write the topic sentence. _____

_____

List the four supporting ideas.

1) _____

2) _____

3) _____

4) _____

Write the closing sentence. _____

_____

 On another piece of paper, use your plan to write an expository paragraph.

Answer Key

Page 5
1. S; 2. F; 3. S; 4. S; 5. F; 6. F;
7. S; 8. F; 9. F; 10. F; 11. S; 12. S

Page 6
1. Some of these things are wood, plants, and nectar. 2. Flower nectar makes good food for bees. 3. Wasps build nests to store their food.
4. Termites are wood eaters.
5. A butterfly caterpillar eats leaves.
6. Mosquitoes bite animals and people.

Page 7
1. One type is called igneous.
2. They are formed by layers of rocks, plants, and animals.
3. Rocks are found everywhere in our world.

Page 8
1. There are three types of rocks on our planet. 2. The melted rock inside the earth is more than 2000°F.
3. Most igneous rocks are formed inside the earth. 4. Marble is a metamorphic rock. 5. Fossils are found in sedimentary rock.

Page 9
1. Why is that car in a tree?
2. Should that monkey be driving a bus? 3. Did you see feathers on that crocodile? 4. Can elephants really lay eggs? 5. Is that my mother covered in spots?

Page 10
Questions will vary.

Page 11
1. period; 2. question mark;
3. period; 4. exclamation point;
5. question mark; 6. period;
7. question mark; 8. period;
9. question mark; 10. exclamation point; 11. period; 12. exclamation point; Bonus: When reading an exclamation, a voice shows strong feeling.

Page 12
1. The Sahara Desert is in Africa.
2. Do people live in the Sahara Desert? 3. The Sahara Desert is about the same size as the United States. 4. How high is the temperature in the Sahara Desert? 5. Once the temperature reached 138°F!

Page 13
Every sentence begins with a capital letter. A statement ends with a period. A question ends with a question mark. An exclamation ends with an exclamation point. Sentences will vary. Bonus: Did it snow ten inches last night? It snowed ten inches last night!

Page 14
   The kids at Elm School had been waiting for a snowstorm. They knew school would be canceled if the storm brought a lot of snow. Last week their wish came true. It snowed 12 inches! School was canceled, and the kids spent the day sledding, building snowmen, and drinking hot chocolate. It was a great snow day! Corrected sentences will vary.

Page 15
D, B, F, E, A, C

Page 16
Sentences will vary.

Page 17
Sentences will vary.

Page 18
Sentences will vary.

Page 19
1. I ordered a hamburger and a milkshake. 2. I like salt and ketchup on my French fries. 3. My mom makes great pork chops and applesauce. 4. My dad eats two huge helpings of meat loaf and potatoes! 5. My brother helps set the table and clean the dishes.
6. We have cookies and ice cream for dessert.

Page 20
1. We are eating out tonight because Mom worked late. 2. We are going to Joe's Fish Shack although I do not like fish. 3. Dad said I can play outside until it's time to leave. 4. We can play video games while we are waiting for our food. 5. We may stop by Ida's Ice Cream Shop after we leave the restaurant.

Page 21
Lists of words will vary.

Page 22
Possible answers: 1. The melting snow cone sat in the bright sun.
2. Many excited children ran toward the crashing ocean waves.
3. My new friends built a large sand castle. 4. My younger brother grabbed his favorite beach toys.
5. Our playful dog tried to catch flying beach balls.

Page 23
Words will vary.

Page 24
Words will vary.

Page 25
Dialogue sentences will vary.

Page 26
1. I think it's fun to splash in the puddles. 2. Rain, rain, don't go away! 3. Wow! I should have worn my bathing suit! 4. It's a perfect day to go sailing.

Page 27
Possible answers: "Somebody turned out the lights!" shouted the cowboy. "What makes you think I've been eating cookies?" asked the guilty boy. "My parents finally let me get my ears pierced," said the proud girl.

Page 28
Drew woke up early on Saturday. "No school today," he said. He found his mom working in the garden. "What are you doing?" he asked.

"I am planting these flowers," she answered.

Drew looked down. He couldn't believe it. "A four-leaf clover!" he shouted. "This should help us win our big game today," he said.

Drew's entire day was perfect. His sister shared her toys, the ice-cream truck brought his favorite flavor, and his team won the big game. "What a day!" he whispered to himself as he fell asleep that night.

Page 29
Sentences will vary.

Page 30
Paragraphs will vary.

Page 31
Lists of ideas will vary.

Page 32
Sentences that do not belong: My favorite kind of dog is a boxer. Not much is known about the history of Chinese flags. Hurricanes have strong, powerful winds.

Page 33
Topic sentences will vary. Possible answers: Guinea pigs make good pets. It is easy to make a peanut butter and banana sandwich. Frogs are different from toads.

Page 34
Topic sentences will vary.

Page 35
The following sentences should be crossed out: My three-year-old brothers both have blonde hair. Her favorite sport is gymnastics. I wish I had a fish tank in my room. The rewritten paragraph should omit the above sentences.

Page 36
Supporting sentences will vary.

Page 37
2, 1, 4, 3; Paragraph sentences will vary but should follow the same order as the numbered sentences.

Page 38
Supporting sentences will vary.

Page 39
1. Of all the seasons, autumn is the best. 2. Though dangerous, the job of an astronaut is exciting. 3. There are many subjects in school, but math is the most difficult. 4. Some gardeners in Florida and Texas can enjoy their flowers all year long. 5. Life would never be the same without computers.

Page 40
Closing sentences will vary.

Page 41
Paragraphs will vary.

Page 42
Paragraph plans and paragraphs will vary.

Page 43
Sentences will vary, and paragraph plans will vary.

Page 44
Drawings and paragraph plans will vary.

Page 45
Paragraph plans and paragraphs will vary.

Page 46
Paragraph plans and paragraphs will vary.